HOW THE WORLD MAKES MUSIC

VOICES AND SINGING

ANITA GANERI

W

FRANKLIN WATTS
LONDON•SYDNEY

 An Appleseed Editions book

First published in 2011 by Franklin Watts
338 Euston Road, London NW1 3BH

Franklin Watts Australia
Hachette Children's Books
Level 17/207 Kent St, Sydney, NSW 2000

© 2011 Appleseed Editions

Created by Appleseed Editions Ltd,
Well House, Friars Hill, Guestling,
East Sussex TN35 4ET

Designed by Guy Callaby
Illustrated by Graham Rosewarne
Edited by Jinny Johnson
Picture research by Su Alexander

ISBN 978-1-4451-0358-7

Dewey Classification: 783

A CIP catalogue for this book is available from the British Library.

Picture credits
l = left, r = right, t = top, b = bottom
Title page l United Archives GmbH/Alamy, cl Rupena/Shutterstock, cr Alistair Scott/Alamy,
r Shutterstock, b Ted Pink Alamy; Contents page Gallo Images/City Press/Alamy; P4 Robert Fried/Alamy;
5 David Fleetham/Alamy; 6 LM &APL/Alamy; 7t Rupena/Shutterstock, b Geoffrey Robinson/Alamy;
8 Robert Harding Picture Library/Alamy; 9 David Lyons/Alamy; 10 Paul Thompson Images/Alamy; 11 Jeff
Morgan 05/Alamy; 12 Harry Hu/Shutterstock; 13 Tan Kian Khoon/Shutterstock; 14 Redferns/Getty
Images; 15 Marshall Ikonography/Alamy; 16 The Art Gallery Collection/Alamy; 17t Only Fabrizio/
Shutterstock, b Isabel Benchetrit/Alamy; 18 Dinodia Images/Alamy; 19t Shutterstock, b Davinder Sangha/
Alamy; 20 Gallo Images/City Press/Alamy; 21t Robert Harding Picture Library/Alamy, b Suzanne Porter/
Alamy; 22 Picture Contact BV/Alamy; 23t Ted Pink/Alamy, b Network Photographers/Alamy; 24 Tom
Allwood/Alamy; 25 Alistair Scott/Alamy; 26 KST Images/Alamy; 27t Pictorial Press Ltd/Alamy, b
INTERFOTO/Alamy; 28 Pictorial Press Ltd/Alamy; 29 United Archives GmbH/Alamy; 30 Robert Fried/
Alamy; 31 Jeff Morgan 05/Alamy:

Front cover: main image Alamy/United Archives GmbH; background image Dmitro2009/Shutterstock;
top row (left to right) Faraways/Shutterstock; Testing/Shutterstock; Ledoct/Shutterstock; Birute
Vijeikiene/Shutterstock

Printed in Singapore

Franklin Watts is a division of Hachette Children's Books,
an Hachette UK company.
www.hachette.co.uk

Contents

Voices and singing

People all over the world make music. They play musical instruments and sing songs when they are happy or sad, and as part of festivals and other ceremonies. People enjoy listening to music as they go about their daily lives.

In many places, such as Africa (below), singing plays an important part in people's lives. People sing to tell stories and show their feelings.

Vocal cords relaxed during breathing

Vocal cords taut when making sound

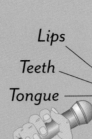

Throat

Lips

Vocal cords

Teeth

Tongue

Larynx (voice box)

Trachea (windpipe)

The human voice

This book is about the voice. We use our voices for speaking and singing. The larynx (voice box) sits in the top of the trachea (windpipe). Two bands of muscle and tissue, called the vocal cords, stretch across it. When you speak or sing, you breathe out and air passes over the vocal cords, pulling them tight so that they vibrate and produce sounds. These sounds are shaped by your lips, teeth, tongue and face muscles.

Musical Notes

The blue whale has the loudest voice of any animal. Its call can reach an incredible 188 decibels – louder than a jet plane (140 decibels) and twice as loud as an opera singer (80 – 90 decibels). The sound can travel for thousands of kilometres underwater.

Types of voice

In Western classical music, singing voices are grouped by different types. These are based on how high or low singers can sing, their vocal range, and the sound of their voices.

Female voices

● **Soprano** – the highest female voice. Sopranos have bright, clear voices and often sing the lead parts in choirs and operas.

● **Mezzo-soprano** – the most common female voice, with a deeper, fuller sound.

● **Contralto** – the lowest female voice, with a richer, heavier sound.

Apart from having a good voice, you need to practise for years if you want to become a top classical singer.

Male voices

● **Countertenor** – the highest male voice, with a bright, light sound.

● **Tenor** – a voice that can be light and bright, or warm and dramatic.

● **Baritone** – the most common male voice with a deeper, heavier tone.

● **Bass** – the lowest male voice and the lowest voice type. Bass voices are deep and booming.

The famous Italian tenor, Luciano Pavarotti, singing in 2005.

Musical Notes

Boy singers whose voices have not yet broken are called trebles. They have high, clear voices and often sing the highest parts in choirs. They are sometimes called boy sopranos.

Singing in a choir

A choir is a group of singers who perform together. Music that is written for choirs to perform is called choral music. Choirs can perform all kinds of music, from religious to popular.

Choirs give special performances of carols and festive songs at Christmas.

Choral singing

Some people sing in choirs professionally. They are able to sing in tune, follow the conductor and sight-read music. Other people take part just for fun. All choral singers must learn to sing together, with each voice performing its part at the right time. Choirs are often mixed, with male and female singers.

A professional choir from Wales. The conductor stands in front, facing the choir.

Choir structure

Many choral works are written for four voices – soprano, alto, tenor and bass (see pages 30–31). These four voices sing together in harmony. In some works, individual singers perform a solo. The choir may be accompanied by a piano or organ, a full orchestra, or by no instruments at all. It is led by a conductor, or choirmaster who stands in front of the singers.

Musical Notes

Some choirs are enormous. In May 2009, a choir of at least 10,000 people took part in a sing-along in the Indian city of Hyderabad.

Opera

An opera is a type of play in which the characters sing their lines rather than speak them. Words and music are used together to tell a story, in an exciting spectacle of music, drama and dance.

Opera story

Opera was first performed in Italy more than 400 years ago. It soon spread to the rest of Europe and specially designed opera houses were built. Some of the greatest composers of opera included Mozart, Wagner, Verdi and Puccini.

The famous Opéra in Paris, France. This beautiful opera house opened in 1875 and has seats for 2,200 people

Opera singers

The singers who perform the leading roles in an opera are called the principals. Often a soprano and tenor sing the roles of the hero and heroine. There is also a chorus, made up of soprano, alto, tenor and bass voices (see pages 30–31). Becoming an opera singer takes years of training. Among other things, singers have to learn to 'project' their voices naturally so that even the quietest notes can be heard by the audience.

Singers from the Welsh National Opera performing an opera by Mozart.

Musical Notes

Here are some of the words used in opera:

● **Aria** – *a solo sung to express a character's feelings.*

● **Leitmotif** – *a short piece of music played whenever a particular character, place or idea appears.*

● **Libretto** – *the words or story of an opera.*

● **Recitative** – *part of the text that tells the audience about the plot. It is sung in a speech-like way.*

● **Score** – *the music for an opera.*

Chinese opera

Chinese opera is a type of musical theatre that began as long ago as the 3rd century and is still very popular in China today. Audiences enjoy a noisy spectacle of song and dance, acting, poetry, acrobatics, storytelling and martial arts.

A group of Chinese opera singers, showing off their fabulous costumes and make-up. The costumes tell the audience who the characters are.

Beijing opera

In Beijing opera, one type of Chinese opera, stories are based on legends and on historical and modern-day events. The performers half-speak and half-sing the words. They use mime gestures and facial expressions to show what is happening in the plot. The performance is accompanied by musicians playing traditional Chinese string and percussion instruments.

Costumes and make-up

Performers in Chinese opera wear magnificent costumes, wigs and headdresses. Heroes tend to wear simpler costumes. Evil or higher ranking characters wear more elaborate clothes. Different styles and colours of make-up are used for the different characters. From these, the audience can tell at once which characters are which and what they are like.

Throat singing

Throat singing is traditionally performed by the Inuit of North America. It was sung by women to entertain their children while the men were away on hunting trips. It was seen as more of a game or contest than a type of music.

Today, some singers specialise in performing a mixture of throat singing and pop music. Tanya Tagaq has developed her own solo form of throat singing.

The singers make the sounds by breathing in and out.

Musical Notes

The sounds used by singers can be actual Inuit words or made-up sounds. These are often the sounds of animals, birds or running water, which are common in everyday life.

Singing a duet

Usually, two women stand facing each other. They may shuffle from one foot to another as they sing. One singer leads, while the other responds. The leader makes a rhythmical pattern of short, breathy sounds. She pauses, then repeats the song, then pauses again and so on. Each time she pauses, the other singer fills in the gap. The first person to run out of breath or laugh loses the game. Some singers can keep going for to 20 minutes.

Chanting

Chanting is a way of half-singing, half-speaking sounds to a steady, even rhythm. Chants are sung in many religions. People chant prayers and passages from the sacred texts as part of their worship. They are not usually accompanied by music.

Gregorian chant

For centuries, parts of the Roman Catholic Mass and other services have been chanted. Gregorian chant, named after Pope Gregory, dates back to the 7th century when monks learned chants by heart. Psalms and prayers are also chanted. Sometimes, only a few notes are used, but several melodies may be chanted at once.

An illuminated manuscript from the 13th century, showing St Gregory. He gave his name to Gregorian chant.

Musical Notes

Some Buddhists chant hundreds of mantras a day. They use strings of beads to help them concentrate and keep count.

Buddhist chanting

As part of their worship, many Buddhists chant sacred words, called 'mantras'. They chant the mantra out loud or quietly to themselves. They believe that chanting mantras helps to open up their minds.

One very famous mantra is 'Om mani padme hum' which means 'Om, the jewel in the lotus'.

Indian voices

There are many different Indian singing styles and songs, from classical to folk to pop. Music plays a very important part in the lives of people in India, especially in religious worship and entertainment.

Songs of worship

During ceremonies in Hindu mandirs (temples), worshippers sing songs, called bhajans. Singing is a way for people to show their devotion to God. The songs are accompanied by musical instruments, such as drums and hand-cymbals. Singers clap along in time with the music.

As part of worship, an Indian sadhu (priest) sings bhajans and other religious songs.

18

Movie music

'Filmi' music is songs from Indian films. It is the most popular type of music in India, where films often feature six or seven songs. The songs are not usually sung by the actors and actresses themselves. They are recorded beforehand by playback singers. Then the actors mime the words in front of the cameras.

Indian films are packed with song and dance. These have become popular around the world.

Bhangra beat

Bhangra is a lively mix of music and dance from the Punjab in northwest India. Traditionally, it was performed at harvest festivals but today it is famous all over the world. Performers wear colourful costumes and are accompanied by the beat of drums. A singer sings folk songs and also shouts encouragement at the dancers.

Musical Notes

Rabindranath Tagore (1861 – 1941), a great Indian poet, wrote more than 2,000 songs, including the national anthem of India.

Bhangra is popular in India and in other countries, such as Britain, where Indian people have gone to live.

African voices

In Africa, there is a huge range of singing styles. One is isicathamiya, which is a singing style from the Zulu people of South Africa. It is sung by groups of singers whose voices blend together. There is no musical accompaniment. Isicathamiya was traditionally sung by groups of men who left their homes to find work in the cities.

The group Ladysmith Black Mambazo has made isicathamiya singing known worldwide. The group became famous when it worked with American musician, Paul Simon, on his 1986 album Graceland.

Griot singing

Griots are poets and singers from West Africa. They sing songs about the history of their people, current events and politics. The griot tradition is thousands of years old and is passed on from one generation to the next. Long ago, each village had its own griot and griots also travelled with warriors and kings.

Being a griot can be passed down in a family. Songs are passed on by word of mouth.

Berber music

The Berber people of Morocco have a style of folk singing called ahwash. The singers form two large choruses that sing in a call-and-response style. This means that one group sings a line which is repeated or answered by the other group. The choruses may be hundreds of singers strong, and are accompanied by drums and flutes.

A group of Berber women in Morocco, singing traditional songs.

Gospel music

Gospel music is religious music that carries a Christian message. Gospel songs are written to praise and thank God. They are sung in a lively and energetic way, and may be performed in churches or in concert halls. Many pop singers have been influenced by gospel sounds.

How gospel began

Gospel was first sung hundreds of years ago in the southern USA. It began with the songs sung by African slaves as they worked in the fields and plantations. These sometimes contained hidden messages of hope and freedom. Also important were the hymns they sang in church.

A gospel choir singing in a church in Memphis, USA. Singers may dance, clap and sway along to the music.

Gospel choirs

Singing is a very important part of gospel music. Singers usually perform in choirs, and sing in harmony or in unison (together). Some singers sing solos. The singers are accompanied by a piano or organ, drums and guitars. Songs are catchy and tuneful, with a strong chorus. Today, gospel choirs, such as the Harlem Gospel Choir from the USA, give performances around the world.

Strong tunes and harmonies are important parts of gospel music. Choirs often include male and female voices.

Musical Notes

In 1996, the London Community Gospel Choir was nominated for the Oscar for Best Original Song for its version of 'Circle of Life', part of the soundtrack for the hit film The Lion King.

Qawwali

Qawwali are traditional songs sung by Sufi Muslims in Pakistan and India. They date back hundreds of years. The songs are mostly sung in the Urdu or Punjabi languages, and are a way of showing the singer's love for and devotion to Allah (God).

Qawwali singing

Qawwali are usually performed by a group of musicians – a lead singer, backing singer, chorus, drummers and harmonium players. They sit cross-legged on the ground. A song starts off slowly and quietly, and gradually gets faster and faster. The audience also join in.

Qawwali singers at a Muslim shrine in Delhi, India. Qawwali has also become popular around the world and Qawwali singers sometimes appear at music festivals.

Yodelling

Yodelling is a special way of singing without words. The singer sings one, long note but keeps switching between using his normal voice and a falsetto (very high) voice. This produces a warbling, song-like sound. It is heard in Swiss folk music, American country and western music, and in some music from the Middle East and Africa.

Keeping in touch

It is thought that yodelling was originally used in Switzerland for people, such as cowherds and goatherds, to be able to communicate in the mountains. By yodelling in places that would produce an echo, they were able to send sounds across long distances. Today, yodelling is mostly heard in folk festivals and on recordings.

Yodellers in Switzerland. Their voices keep switching between high-low-high-low sounds.

Country, blues and jazz

Country, blues and jazz are three types of music that began in the USA. All three have become very popular around the world and are often mixed with rock and pop music.

Country

Country music began in rural, farming areas of the southern USA. It was broadcast on the radio in the 1920s and soon became hugely popular. Country songs often tell sad stories about lost love, loneliness or poverty. Singers sing alone, or in duets, and often accompany themselves on the guitar.

Alison Krauss is an American country singer. She recently made an album with Robert Plant, the lead singer of legendary rock band, Led Zeppelin.

Blues

The Blues grew from the work songs of the African-American communities of the southern USA in the late 19th century. The songs use slightly off-pitch notes and they express feelings, usually of sadness and longing, instead telling a story. Singers may be accompanied by the piano, harmonica, drums and guitar.

Musical Notes

One of greatest jazz and blues singers of all time was American, Billie Holiday (1915 – 1959). When she sang the song 'Body and Soul' in a nightclub, she reduced the audience to tears.

Jazz

Like the blues, jazz began in the southern USA and has now spread across the world. A jazz band often has a singer, with trumpets, saxophones, drums, piano and double bass. An important feature of jazz is improvisation. This is the way that singers and musicians take the melody, then alter it to make up their own tune.

Louis Armstrong was famous for his rich, raspy voice. He often sang with sounds instead of words.

Reggae, hip-hop and rap

Reggae

Reggae began in Jamaica in the late 1960s. Based on a lively rhythm, it has a strong beat for dancing. The singer is accompanied by various instruments, especially the drums and bass guitar which play the rhythm and give a thick, heavy sound. One of the greatest figures in reggae was Bob Marley (1945 – 1981), who sang with his group, the Wailers.

Bob Marley, performing with the Wailers and his backing singers, the I Threes. Marley played guitar and was lead singer and songwriter.

Hip-hop

Hip-hop is a whole lifestyle, based around a type of music which began in New York in the 1970s. Its edgy lyrics tell of young people's struggles to find jobs and fit into society. Hip-hop has been criticised for sometimes being too violent or aggressive.

Rapping

A rapper, or MC, speaks or chants the words of a song, in time to a beat. The words are often spoken very quickly, in rhyme or verse. A rapper must have a strong, clear voice and good breathing technique. Music is provided by a DJ, live band, drum machine or synthesiser.

Missy Elliott is one of the top female rappers in the world. Her first album, **Supa Dupa Fly** *was a massive hit.*

Here are some of the words used in hip-hop:

● *Sampling: taking part of a piece of music and using it in another piece of music.*

● *Scratching: when a DJ moves a* vinyl record back and forth on a turntable.

● *Beatboxing: making the sound of drum beats, using the mouth, lips, tongue and voice.*

● *Looping: taking a short piece of music and repeating it.*

● *Breakdancing: athletic style of dancing to hip-hop music.*

Words to remember

alto
Short for contralto. The lowest female or highest adult male voice.

bass
The lowest adult male voice.

Buddhist
A person who follows the teaching of the Buddha, a holy man who lived in India thousands of years ago.

choir
An organised group of singers.

decibels
A unit measuring how loud a sound is.

harmony
A combination of notes that are sung or played at the same time.

Hindu
A person who follows the ancient Indian religion of Hinduism.

Inuit
The Inuit are people who have lived in the Arctic for thousands of years.

larynx
The voice box in the throat.

mime
The telling of a story using movements instead of words.

Mozart
German Wolfgang Amadeus Mozart (1756 – 1791) was one of the greatest composers of classical music, writing more than 600 works.

Puccini
Giacomo Puccini (1858 – 1924) was an Italian composer who wrote many famous operas, including *La Bohème* and *Madame Butterfly*.

soprano
The highest adult female voice.

Sufi
A Sufi is a Muslim (follower of the religion of Islam) who believes in using music and dance to feel closer to Allah (God).

tenor
The second highest adult male voice, below a countertenor.

trebles
Boys whose voices have not yet broken and who have high, clear voices.

Verdi
Giuseppe Verdi (1813 – 1901) was an Italian composer of operas and other choral works, including *Rigoletto* and *Aida*.

vocal cords
Two bands of muscle and tissue stretched across the voice box.

Wagner
German composer, Richard Wagner (1813 – 1883), is famous for his dramatic works, including *The Ring of the Nibelung* which is made up of four operas.

Index